Yoga Wisdom

Reflections of a Practicing Yogi

Anita Perry

Copyright © 2018 by **Anita Perry**

All rights reserved. No part of this publication may be reproduced, distributed or transmitted in any form or by any means, without prior written permission.

YogaAnita, LLC
Leominster, MA 01453
www.yogaanita.com

Yoga Wisdom/ Anita Perry. -- 1st ed.
ISBN 978-0-692-08978-1

Dedicated to all my yoga students:
past, present, future

Contents

Introduction 1

Choosing the Yoga for You 5

Yoga for Couples 9

5 Top Reasons for Doing Yoga Now! 13

You Can Relax in Yoga! 17

Put Yoga in Schools! 21

The Yoga of Technology 25

Watertown Pride 31

The Boston Marathon-A Year Later 35

Yoga Yamas-Ahimsa 41

The Yoga Truth 45

What's Stealing Your Time? 49

No Sex in Yoga? 53

Yoga for Obama 57

Tied Up in Knots? 61

Be Free With Yoga 65

Yoga and Death 69

Warm Up With Yoga 73

Making Time for Yoga 77

Not Your Average Yoga 81

Yoga in A Blizzard 85

A Yoga Valentine For You 89

5 Ways to Discover Yoga 93

Yoga for Depression 97

Back to School Yoga 101

Yoga for Job Loss 103

What is Yoga Nidra? 109

Being Thankful and Content! 113

Don't Go Strapless in Yoga! 117

Discounted Senior? 121

Karma Yoga-Not Karma Sutra! 127

Yoga and McDonald's 131

Sssh! I Do It Everywhere!....................... 135

Being in Easy Pose When the Mind is Not 139

Bringing Yoga On Vacation 143

Olympic Lessons For The Rest of Us 147

Preparing for (A) Fall in Yoga 151

Practicing Kindness 155

It's Not OK! 159

Can You Really Be Thankful? 163

• CHAPTER 1 •

Introduction

When I took my first yoga class in college, I did not like it. In fact, you could say, I really disliked it. After all, I was an aerobic instructor and trainer. I was used to the fast paced, feel the burn, sweat drenching excitement of a cardio workout punctuated with a pulsating bass line and snappy pop tunes. I did not want to sit still, cross-legged on a mat, "expanding my consciousness". I had places to go and people to see, and while the end of the class was relaxing, I did not take yoga seriously.

Fast forward 30 years later, to a series of repetitive stress injuries, sore hips and knees, and a demanding life and yoga started to look a little better. So much so, that I made yoga my primary form of exercise. Eventually I found my way into a teacher training program and I was ready to immerse myself- body and mind-into this practice.

As I delved deeper into the study of yoga, I first noticed the physical effects. I seemed more flexible. My aches and pains slowly diminished. I was sleeping better. If I got an injury, it didn't last as long. I learned to self heal. Beyond the physical, I was able to face difficult situations calmly, find peace and beauty in my everyday surroundings, set goals and stick to them.

And when I was able to share that with my students, I found my calling. Since my form of expression is in educating, instructing, and writing, I started sharing my message in articles, blog posts, and in my book, ***Yogaminute***.

This book is a collection of blog posts and articles that I was inspired to write as aspects of yoga revealed itself to me. Some of them are dated to reflect the news of the day, but the wisdom is still there. Feel free to skip around and see what speaks to you. It is not meant to be sequential. I hope it inspires you to seek how yoga can fit into your life.

• CHAPTER 2 •

Choosing the Yoga for You

January is the time that many people are looking to get started in a fitness regimen. Cardio and weight training used to be the norm, but in the last few years, more people are asking me about yoga to meet their fitness goals. I am happy to see the spread of yoga into the mainstream, but since the practice of yoga has been westernized and commercialized, there are some misconceptions out there that I'd like to address.

First, there are many types of yoga and you need to find the tradition that suits your personality and fitness goals. If you are looking for a vigorous workout, try a vinyasa flow or a power yoga class. If you are recovering from an injury, look at hot yoga or restorative yoga. If you like routine, try a bikram class. If you are looking to deepen your practice with meditation involved, go for hatha or anusara.

Second, find a class with trained instructors. Looking good in leggings and sporting an "ohm" tattoo does not a good instructor make. Investigate by asking for recommendations; look at an instructor's reviews on their website, or Facebook, and check out the directory at yogaalliance.org which is the premiere certifying organization for yoga professionals.

Third, realize that the movement (asana) is just one facet of yoga. If that is your main goal, then you probably can find a yoga class at your local gym or Y. But if you are looking to incorporate the deeper practice of a yoga lifestyle, than you would be better served in a Center that specializes in yoga.

Finally, realize that nothing in yoga should ever hurt or make you feel uncomfortable. Choosing the yoga practice that resonates with you might take some time, but it is so worth it. I have had students who have started with me go on to other practices and then loyal students who have been with me for years. I cherish both because their experiences make me a better instructor.

I hope that you consider adding yoga as part of a healthy lifestyle and find the practice that enhances your enjoyment and quality of life. It is so worth it!

• CHAPTER 3 •

Yoga for Couples

Love to do yoga? How about sharing it with your spouse or your significant other? We all know how beneficial yoga can be for your body, your mind, and your spirit-now, think of that times two! Here are some ideas to get you motivated to try yoga as a duo!

1. Set a Time

As a couple, you can set a time to be together. Put it on your calendar and send a reminder text letting your honey know you are spending this special time just with him/her!

2. Set a place

If you are beginners, go to a studio to get the proper instruction, but practice at home together. The bedroom is a great place to do yoga. The final pose is savasana after all, and what better way to do this pose than in bed!

3. Set an Intention

Meditation is a big part of your yoga practice and setting an intention lays the groundwork for a deeper, more concentrated practice. Establishing a mutual intention with your partner creates a shared goal and lasting bond.

What poses should you do as a couple? The field is wide open if you are an experienced yogi and using each other as a "prop" allows for deeper stretching. However, unless you are a trained professional, I wouldn't recommend hands on assists or over stretching. Also it important to refrain from giving "advice" to your partner during yoga, which could lead to physical injury and discord within the relationship. Start by developing a mutual breathing pattern and choosing a set of poses that you know. Always start with a warmup and end with your final resting pose. In yoga, as with most things, quality is always more important than quantity.

You will find as you progress through your shared yoga practice, a greater appreciation for the physical, mental, and spiritual benefits will follow. This can lead to a more fulfilling, intimate relationship. Yoga is good for one; fantastic for two! Give it a try today!

• CHAPTER 4 •

5 Top Reasons for Doing Yoga Now!

Have you heard this old joke?
　　　　Q. If April Showers bring May flowers, what do May flowers bring?
　　　　A. Pilgrims!

In my yoga practice, April, rather than January, seems to be the month of yoga pilgrims. Perhaps it is because I live in the cold Northeast, and winter seems to make everyone but the hardy hibernate but April is my highest month of new students, many of whom are trying yoga for the first time. These new students, like pilgrims, are seekers. Some are seeking the physical-flexibility, relief from pain, or a low impact workout. Others are seeking the spiritual-calm, peace, tranquility, or enlightenment. Some are looking to follow the latest fad (yes, yoga is now main streamed), some think they'll meet a hot guy (or girl) in class. Here's what you can expect should you decide to start a yoga practice:

1. Overall health and vitality in a non-competitive atmosphere, that doesn't care what you look like, where you come from, or how fit you are or aren't
2. A healthful practice that should never, ever, hurt you
3. Better sleep, better sex, better digestion

4.   Increased sense of confidence and self control

5.   A glowing outer and inner you

If this sounds good to you, contact your nearest, certified yoga instructor and make that pilgrimage to yoga today. Your body, your mind, your friends and family will thank you!

• CHAPTER 5 •

You Can Relax in Yoga!

When new students first start taking yoga, I tell them the hardest thing about the class is sitting still. Of all the poses in yoga, sitting still in sukhasana (easy pose) or relaxing in savasana (corpse pose) is the hardest to master. Why? Because you have to give yourself permission to be quiet! Quieting the body might be achievable but quieting the mind? Even with the best of intentions, all these thoughts start to intrude, the mind starts replaying the day's events (in yoga it's actually called the monkey mind) chattering endlessly on and on until the last thing you want to do is be sitting in yoga class! How do we quiet the mind as well as the body?

The simplest answer to that is to breathe. By concentrating on your breath, even counting the breaths to yourself as you inhale and exhale, helps you to refocus. Repeating a simple phrase or a non-sensical humming sound also helps. For instance, if you are of the Kundalini tradition, you would know to chant Sat Nam or Sat Ta Na Ma as part of your meditation. Other yoga traditions have certain chants, hums, or sounds as well. However, it is not necessary to devote yourself to learning these unless you have a keen interest in the spiritual aspect of your practice. Simply cleansing the mind by breathing, focusing on a concentration point, or closing the eyes, is enough for most.

Another thing to try is the use of an eye pillow, especially if the pillow contains the soothing herb lavender. Imagine being covered head to toe with a comfy blanket and then having a pillow resting on your eyes. Instant relaxation! I personally use the essential oil and place a few drops on my wet hair. It just sets the tone for your entire day.

In this frantic, hectic, overloaded world, having the tools to be calm and relaxed are essential. You owe it to yourself and the people around you.

CHAPTER 6

Put Yoga in Schools!

Spring is almost here and that means it's time for what I call "Test Insanity". Schools around the country are preparing their students to take standardized tests by doing endless practice tests, drills, and targeted instruction designed to give students an edge in the test. In Massachusetts, we are also introducing the computerized PARCC Test and MCAS 2.0, which require instruction in keyboarding and computer applications. For months, the teachers, specialists, and literacy coaches have been talking about this test. Though the students are told, "Just do your best", there is an underlying hint of hysteria as harried and already overwhelmed teachers try to fit in one more thing into their daily schedules.

This past week, I was honored to present at a test preparation assembly, but my preparation technique involved breathing, being quiet, and calming the body. Students were introduced to simple breathing, mindfulness, and stretching that help to calm the body and mind. I feel that this skill is not only a useful strategy for test preparation but also a life skill for the challenges beyond. Why does yoga need to be in schools? Yoga can:

- Help students to self regulate using simple breathing techniques
- Help decrease anxiety and nervousness
- Teach non-violence, honesty, and service to others
- Promote self confidence
- Teach students to set goals

And of course there is the added benefit of increasing strength and flexibility and teaching healthy living.

The beauty of incorporating yoga into our schools is that it doesn't require a lot of space or special equipment or even a time commitment. I provide twenty-minute yoga breaks at my current school right in the classrooms, - no mats, chanting, or incense required! Everyone has responded positively and the students are eager to show me what they have learned as I pass them in the hallway or see them in the cafeteria and playground.

If we have to tack on "one more thing" into our curriculum, let's make it a positive, enriching experience. More yoga, less tests!

• CHAPTER 7 •

The Yoga of Technology

I consider myself an educated person. I have a Master's Degree in Education and have used technology since the days of the Wang word processor (If you remember that-let me know!) I've successfully integrated technology into my classroom and have used technology and social media to get the public educated into the ways of yoga. When it works- it's great! When it doesn't...

Let me begin last Sunday. My old flip phone that I use for business is coming up for renewal. Why not upgrade to a newer phone, I thought. So online I go to research phones, saw one at Walmart for an excellent price, ran it by my son for his opinion ("Looks OK") and off I went to get it. I successfully transferred my minutes and phone number to the new phone and turned it on. Then I started reentering my contact info. (Isn't there an easier way to do that?) Three hours later, I found that I hated this new phone! It was not friendly. It was not easy. I wanted my old phone back. Thus began the NIGHTMARE OF THE OLD FLIP PHONE. I could not transfer it online. I could not reach a live person on the customer service line, no matter how many times I dialed. I even tried the Spanish option, hastily trying to get the translation of my problem while waiting for the next representative (which was a phone prompt again-not a real person). I finally reached a chat line agent who advised me that my phone had a problem (Huh?) and would be out of order until I received a new SIM card.

While I was on hold waiting for the phone teleprompter, I noticed that my website had an error in the footer. Why not just update that while I am on hold? But wait-where is the option to do that? It was there a few months ago. So I began my frantic search for the right menu option, and the internal chatter that accompanies situations like these i.e. "Where is it? Why can't I find it? I know I've done this before. What's wrong with me?" And thus was added the sequel RETURN OF TECHNOLOGY WOES (see woman flip out when her phone and website both are not working! Hear the anguished screams of frustration! Not for the faint of heart-tune in if you dare!) The upshot of all of this was more time spent in a phone queue waiting for the web host technical support, being disconnected after holding for seven minutes, being sent to the wrong department, finally reaching a person who didn't fix the problem, being on hold again, finally reaching another person who said it was a theme error (i.e. Not our fault). This led to me contacting my web person, who said it was a hosting error (i.e. Not my fault) but did offer to fix it and suggest I switch hosts. It's still not 100% fixed yet but getting there.

Throughout all this frustrating technology problems, I had to practice the yoga principle of ahimsa, non-harming, both for myself and for thoughts I was having while trying to deal with things beyond my control. I had to practice many calming breathing techniques, even more when I thought the problem was fixed and then it started all over again a few days later. Perhaps I should take my own advice (See What's Stealing Your Time?), keep sipping my lovely summer alcoholic beverage and thinking calming, cooling, positive thoughts that the technology gods would look favorably upon me soon.

PS. It is now a week later and I'm hold again-seems some application is not working on the phone preventing me from making and receiving phone calls. Breathe in, breathe out...

CHAPTER 8

Watertown Pride

(Published on April 20, 2013 in the aftermath of the Boston Marathon Bombing)

I'm a Watertown, Massachusetts girl. I was born and raised there, graduated Watertown High School, moved back there as an adult, met my husband there, and went back often to visit family and friends. This week I was out of town burying my father in law who also lived over 60 years of his life in Watertown. I don't know what he would have thought of the activity and drama that unfolded in Watertown in the past 24 hours.

It was eerie to turn on the television and see all the places I've known, shopped, and ate in, as part of a background of an international incident. Anderson Cooper was just down the street from where my late father in law lived! My father in law's widow and children could not return to their home after the funeral because of the massive police and media presence. It was frightening, surreal, and strange.

Yet in the midst of that, there is a certain pride. Pride for the person who saw the blood on the tarp covered boat and called it in. Pride for the massive law enforcement personnel who seemed to be working together. Pride for all the Bostonians and suburban residents who obeyed the governor's warning to stay inside. Massive pride for all the Watertown residents who cheered when the law enforcement trucks, buses, and Hummers were exiting.

In yoga there is a yama called Aparigrapha. To practice it means non-judgement. I do not know what leads a 19 year old boy to want to hurt other people so violently. I'm sure that will all come out-ad nauseum-in the weeks and months to come. I do know I am not going to waste energy trying to decipher his motives. Instead, I am sending out healing energy to all the victims and families of the Boston Marathon, as well as the family of MIT police officer Sean Collier.

I'm sure my father in law, with his dry wit and humor, is also proud as well.

CHAPTER 9

The Boston Marathon-A Year Later

(*Published April 21, 2014*)

Last year at this time, I was sipping coffee, enjoying my first day of spring vacation, and watching the preparations for the annual Boston Marathon. As I watched all the preparations, I was inspired to write an article for this blog and published it just as the runners were beginning their long trek. Little did I know that just a few hours later, some of those same runners and their spectators would be changed forever with a senseless act of violence. I and countless others watched the news, transfixed on the endless replaying of the bombs exploding on the Boylston Street finish line, the terse comments of the reporters, the pictures of families running in horror, and the spectators who happened to be in the wrong place at the wrong time. In the days that followed, I was further horrified by the senseless shooting of the MIT security officer, Sean Collier, and then the shoot-em-up and subsequent manhunt in my hometown of Watertown.

Now a year later, the stories of unbelievable courage and sacrifice abound. These stories tell of the people who were injured and endured long months of physical rehabilitation. Then there's the stories of the countless others who happened to be in the right place at the right time. Not just the medical and law enforcement officials, whose jobs demand automatic and unselfish action, but of ordinary people out enjoying an afternoon of fun turned tragically wrong. It great to have a visit by Vice President Biden and good to see the politicians stop fighting long enough to honor these people. It's doubly terrific to celebrate the World Series Champion Boston Red Sox and have them also honor those victims of the Marathon Bombing. But mostly for me, it's a celebration of human goodness, sacrifice, and willingness to be of service to others. We must remember that we share this earth and our actions on it are overreaching.

ANITA PERRY

I am not part of the Boston Marathon race but I am part of the human race. Let's all race towards our peaceful coexistence on our beautiful planet as we celebrate both the anniversary of the bombing and Earth Day this week.

• CHAPTER 10 •

Yoga Yamas-Ahimsa

On the first limb of the yoga tree we have the Yamas. Yamas consist of a series of observances for right living. The first one is ahimsa. Ahimsa means non-violence.

Most people think of violence in our world as a terrorist act, something that happens to "other people" in far off countries. Occasionally we have violence right in our hometowns and neighborhoods. This was painfully clear from the recent Boston Marathon bombing and the manhunt in my hometown of Watertown, MA. All of a sudden violence was up close and personal with the entire horror, sadness, and media outcry that brings.

Then after a few days, attention shifts. The news cycle changes to another bombing, another terrorist act, and another shooting and we are left with the aftermath. Granted, here in the Boston area and beyond, there has been an outpouring of donations, tributes, and editorials. Even the New York Yankees fans supported the Boston Red Sox fans and if that isn't a miracle-what is? But even so, unless violence becomes personal and is inflicted on the individual, the attention shifts. Have we become so conditioned to accept violence as part of our daily lives?

Practicing ahimsa means to consciously accept a non-violent way of thinking and living. This would include all living things, non-living things, and most especially us. Letting someone cut us off without flipping them the bird. Letting someone take the parking space that is two spaces closer to the door. Being mindful that two year olds do cry and act up sometimes in public places. Taking care to protect our habitats and environments. Listening to our bodies when they are stressed, sick, hungry, tired, and sleepy.

Cultivate peace within. Practice ahimsa and you will be improving the world.

CHAPTER 11

The Yoga Truth

The second yama on the yoga tree is satya, which means truthfulness. This concept is pretty easy to understand yet not so easy to put into practice. We all know that as the bard said, "Oh, what a tangled web we weave when first we practice to deceive", that telling a lie is going to make your nose grow and could put you into a pretty embarrassing situation. But how many of us practice satya with ourselves?

Is it really truthful to say you are all right when you are not inside? How many times have you said, "No, that's all right" or "It's OK" when really you are boiling over with real or imagined hurts? How many times have you put the needs of others before your own?

Recently we celebrated Mother's Day. Moms are the queens of self-sacrifice and self-denial because, well, who else is going to do it if we don't? So even though breakfast in bed, flowers, dinner, and gift certificates are nice; they are also easy solutions to our obligation to recognize Mother's Day. As a Mom, what would you really want for Mother's Day? A day out? Peace and quiet reading a book? Shopping without the children? Your husband voluntarily picking up his clothes off the floor? If you practice satya, you will find (after practice I admit) that you are able to start verbalizing your needs and are able to ask for what you need without feeling guilty or having to negotiate a win-lose situation for yourself.

Here's your challenge: Choose something you really want to happen. Say,
" _(person)_____, I want _____(your intention)_____. Can you help me with that?" It does work if you are willing to try. Then do it! No excuses, short of a family emergency should tear you away from what you have stated you want. You will feel lighter and better. I know it's hard so leave a comment or email me if you need moral support. Also let me know how it goes.

Satya-know your truth, see your truth, and speak your truth. It will really set you free!

• CHAPTER 12 •

What's Stealing Your Time?

On the third limb of the yoga yamas is asteya-which means non-stealing. Most people would think about the universal commandment "Thou Shall Not Steal" in all its many forms. It's a tenet we teach our children and we can all agree that it is wrong to take what does not belong to us. Have you ever thought about the things that steal from us, particularly our time?

Bombs away media!

In our modern world we are bombarded with messages and distractions. How many of us scroll through our Facebook news feed with an almost ADHD fashion looking for the more compelling picture, video, or message that will capture out attention? Online marketers pour over analytics to determine at what point a reader will become bored and move on to the next brightest thing. Our obsessions with all that is technical really manifests itself when you see people sitting around scrolling through their devices rather than have a face to face conversation. How many of us have had a meltdown when our computer, blackberry, or cell phone was not working?

It affects our literacy!

I admit I love the convenience and ease of online information. I like the social media, keeping in touch with family and friends, getting news feeds and goofy dog pictures. On the other hand, I am also an educator lamenting with my colleagues the fact that our children don't read or get enough exercise, and their writing has been reduced to twitter like sentence fragments.

Take Action!

As part of your yoga practice this month, see if you can identify all your time stealers. Ask yourself at the end of the day-did I make the best use of the time I was given today?

• CHAPTER 13 •

No Sex in Yoga?

The fourth yama on the yoga tree is Brahmacharya. In standard yogic texts this means celibacy. That's great and works fine works fine if you are not in a committed relationship. For those are us in a relationship whose partners expect more than hand holding, brahmacharya would be interpreted as clean living and/or proper management of sexual energies. When I first was taught this meaning, my first question was *huh?*

Clean living I can get behind but what is proper management of sexual energy?

First comes the obvious-anything used to exploit sexuality, i.e. porn sites, movies, and graphic magazines should be avoided. Thinking about it, those who do engage in these activities do waste a lot of time and energy. But does that mean it's missionary style or nothing?

To me, committed partners use their sexuality to enhance their relationship. As the relationship and the partners grow, so do the many facets of their sexual lives. It ebbs and flows and is forever changing. When practicing brahmacharya, partners are not afraid to express their needs, to give and to take, and feel free to not engage in any unwanted activity without having to fake a headache.

YOGA WISDOM

Yoga practice will enhance your physical enjoyment of sex. Practicing brahmacharya wil elevate your mental enjoyment of sex. Direct your sexual energy into pleasing your partner and watch what happens to you!

CHAPTER 14

Yoga for Obama

(*Published for Presidents Day, 2013*)

Yoga poses for President Obama? This week we celebrate President's Day with car sales and other irrelevant tributes to our US presidents. Wouldn't it be great instead to celebrate yoga in the White House? If I was President Obama's yoga instructor, these are some of the poses I would recommend for him:

1. Sitali Breathing

We all know that practicing sitali breathing is calming to the nervous system. Sitali, meaning cool breath, is a Yoga breathing method that lowers the fire energy. But think how good it would feel for Mr. President to stick out his tongue as he in inhaling all that cool healing breathe?

2. **Warrior Poses** (Virabhadrasana)

There are three to choose from. It does seem silly to have a warrior series in a non-violent yoga asana, but in the Bhagavad-Gita, there is the dialog between two famous and feared warriors, Krishna and Arjuna, set on a battlefield between two great armies spoiling for a fight. Anyway the spiritual warrior is a strength pose and who couldn't use a little extra strength dealing with the Kim Jong-il and the North Koreans? Also the extra added benefit of strengthening the shoulders and arms, and the muscles of the back helps when you are hunched over your desk in endless cabinet meetings.

3. Chair Pose (Utkatasana)

Chair Pose or Utkatasana is another pose I'd recommend to our leader. This one powerful pose strengthens the ankles, thighs, calves, and spine. We do need someone with a strong spine in this job!

4. Twists-Half Lord of Fishes

There are many to choose from, but I would go with Half Lord of Fishes or Ardha Matsyendrasana. Besides having a pose that name you a "lord", it is great to wring out all those toxins built up from too many late night snacks. It also stimulates the digestive fire in the belly that our leader needs to stand in front of Congress.

5. Relaxation Pose (Savasana)

After hours of negotiating, hand shaking, telephone calls, meetings, speeches, and policy making, it be great for our president to settle into the final relaxation yoga pose or savasana. This is probably the hardest pose of all, since the mind thinks it might have released all its tension, yet in quiet we discover areas that need more relaxation. Savasana requires the student to actively "let go" each time. This pose will relax the entire psycho-physiological system and quiet the heart rate and mind.

So I think we should petition for a nonpartisan referendum to bring yoga to President Obama, the rest of the White House and all elected officials. Think about how cool it would be to have a yoga mat with the presidential seal of approval on it!

God Bless America and Om, Shanti.

• CHAPTER 15 •

Tied Up in Knots?

Yoga teacher Max Strom says of yoga that "The goal is not to tie ourselves up in knots. We're already tied in knots. The aim is to untie the knots in our heart." I don't personally know Mr. Strom but boy am I thinking about his advice as I am writing this blog this week.

Two hours ago, I was resting on my yoga mat, just completing an online video with Rodney Yee. For some reason, I choose the Relaxation Module. I don't know why. After all I was on vacation from my full time teaching job and with more snow on the way, it looks like I'll have even an extra day to relax. Yes, I did do everything I planned to do during this time: doctor's appointments, visiting my yoga school and teacher, on line tutorials, web page updating, volunteer work, thorough cleaning of the house (including cat box), business telephone calls, Facebook updates, meetings at town hall (no I can't build a yoga studio in my back yard because of zoning but I can build a funeral home!), meeting at the bank, errands for my husband, teaching my yoga classes at night, trying some new recipes. This isn't anything that would cause stress, right?

Obviously, yes. As I was getting up off my mat to roll it up thinking about what I had to download off the computer, what I was going to write this week and a dinner engagement this evening, all of a sudden my back would not cooperate. It froze. It locked. It hurt! I couldn't move.

So here I am two hours later, with an ice pack on my back, ibuprofen in my blood stream, and my dog resting against my leg to comfort me. All I can do is breathe, sit, and let my husband and kids help me. Hmmmmm.....

CHAPTER 16

Be Free With Yoga

So I am picking up where I left off from my last post-where I was literally tied up in knots. Even after a week of school "vacation", obviously my body was not at rest and it told me so in a very jarring way. Even more painful was the fact that I had to cancel dinner plans with some good friends who in a little while will be moving back to their native Columbia and won't be just a 5-minute drive anymore.

One of the niymamas or personal practices in yoga is called Svadhyaya. This is a sanskrit word which means introspection and study. As I had plenty of time on the couch with my heating pad and dog to reflect on my painful predicament, I realized that I needed to let go. I needed to step away from the specter of my mother telling me in word and deed what makes a "good" wife/mother (a sparkling clean house and the last person to flop exhausted into bed). I needed to embrace the fact that I actually needed help and that it was OK to sit and do nothing. I needed to evaluate what is truly important and what no longer serves me or is holding me back.

I do not like having muscle spasms but I do like the freedom that comes with deciding which things are the most important and that I can say no without regrets to things that I don't have to or want to do. Too bad it's taken over 50 years to learn this but I'm going to embrace this now.

CHAPTER 17

Yoga and Death

(Published January 14, 2013)

Benjamin Franklin said, "The only things certain in life are death and taxes." This week I experienced two deaths: the death of a dear aunt and the death of a brilliant mind. My dear aunt was inevitable and though we will miss her gentle humor, her faith, and her artistic talents, she has been in declining health for a few years. That, coupled with the death of her husband a few years ago, put her passing in the "blessing" category.

The death of a brilliant mind however, was a shock and completely unexpected. My father in law, a brilliant retired professor of British History, fell during the holidays and is now in a rehab center to assess and provide physical therapy. Though my husband and I had seen some signs of forgetfulness in past conversations, we chocked it up to the usual aging process and did not feel worried. So we were totally unprepared when we visited him in the rehab center. He is a person unknown to us now. Someone who had no concept of time and space, was confused about his surroundings and the medical personnel, and was babbling about things so foreign to us was a shock and a mind opener. We are still reeling trying to process how this could have happened and navigating through the aftermath of an uncertain future ahead. How will his illness progress? What are the options for care, medication, quality of life? And selfishly, how will this affect our lives and us?

How does this fit into an essay about yoga? I really had to practice yoga breathing and principles when I was dealing with both these situations this week. I am grateful for my little yoga breaks I squeeze in and the asanas that provide opening, release, and clarity. I am grateful for the little things that provide a smile (like my dog), a good meal for sustenance, good friends for companionship, and savasana for total relaxation. I am ready for the certain and uncertain things in my life.

• CHAPTER 18 •

Warm Up With Yoga

Baby, it's cold outside! Our whole country is immersed in a deep freeze and so are our bodies. The cold weather wrecks havoc not just on our skin (the largest organ in our body) but also our minds and our spirits. Are you finding that you just don't want to go anywhere but home? Are you avoiding the things you love because it's just too cold? Here's two yoga remedies that can help!

Breathing

Yogic breathing can help to not only calm your body, but, with twists, re-oxygenate your inner organs. Directed three part breathing, known as the dirga pranayama, helps you become aware of your breath and direct the flow of prana, or life force. The three parts are the abdomen, diaphragm, and chest. During Three-Part Breath, you first completely fill your belly, ribcage, and upper chest with air. Then you exhale completely, reversing the flow. I like to close my eyes and actually visualize the air flowing in and flowing out. Give it a try if you feel comfortable.

Self Massage

Massage therapy has so many benefits including increased circulation, calming of nerves, lubrication of the joints, softer skin, and better sleep. My favorite self-indulgence is to get a professional massage. But when you are too cold to go anywhere, you can still do self massage therapy on your own at home. Go into the bathroom, take off all your clothes, and stand on a warm rug. (I added that because I don't like cold feet!) Using oils, a brush, a loofa, or just your hands, start vigorously massaging your arms and legs in long strokes. Don't forget your to include your hands and fingers as well. Then sit down to do your feet-bottoms, ankles, instep, and toes. Afterwards take a warm shower and feel how good you feel! You might even want to get into your yoga gear and go out and take a class!

Take a few moments to take time for you and remember spring is coming soon!

• CHAPTER 19 •

Making Time for Yoga

"We must use time wisely and forever realize that time is always ripe to do things right"- Nelson Mandela (1918-2013)

This is the time of year when we look within and without and set intentions for the upcoming year. Most people start off January with very good intentions-a new job, a relationship overhaul, new healthy living guidelines, and maybe aspiring to something like a new car or living situation as well. These are all worthwhile goals. But ask most people in March how many of these goals have been started and the hands go down. We all have great intentions-but sticking to them is difficult. Our attention span is naturally shortened by the media blasts around us. If we do not receive immediate results, we go on to the next shiny thing. So then, what can we do when we know we need to change something big in our lives?

Redefine and think small.

That's right, think small. Instead of wishing to lose twenty pounds and being overwhelmed with all the diet and exercise that involves, redefine your goal into small, manageable steps. Further, while some people could handle a daily goal, you might be one of those people who might need to send yourself hourly reminders. What should you remind yourself?

> *"I am important and in order to be happy, I will be true to myself"*

It sounds simple, but in real life, how many of us put ourselves first? If you truly put your happiness first in your life, then everything else will fall into place. This is not being selfish or self absorbed but rather loving yourself enough to want the best for yourself. As the commercial says, "You're worth it!"

CHAPTER 20

Not Your Average Yoga

A few weeks ago two young women showed up a few minutes before my yoga class and announced that they were here for "the yoga". I love welcoming new students but I could tell right away that they were probably in for something that they didn't expect, starting with the fact that they glared at me when I asked them to remove their shoes outside the door and to turn off any electronic devices.

They barely glanced at the stack of yoga props I offered (blocks, extra mats, blankets and straps) and settled themselves as far away from me as possible. They eyed me suspiciously when I asked everyone to come to quiet and to breathe deeply. They moved through their practice as if they were getting points for being the fastest, secretly looking at the other students in the class and smiling when they could extend their legs higher or balance longer. By the time it was savasana, I could see they were eyeing the exit doors and sure enough, they beat a very hasty retreat before the last "namaste" was uttered. I doubt that they will be back any time soon.

The popularity of yoga in this country is a double-edged sword. Yes, it introduces potential students to the fact that there is an alternative healthy way of living and moving the body. But it also popularizes an unreal expectation, clad in Lululemon and bending into unrealistic poses. Yoga is so much more than that. *Yoga is not what you do on the mat, but off of it.*

Believe me, I do not fault those two young women because I was just like them when I was their age. I didn't think I worked hard enough unless I was feeling the "burn" and/or sporting an ace bandage on an injury like a badge of courage. But hours in the gym and counting fat grams did not make me a better person. Only being older, wiser, and studying yoga helped to set me on the right path to inner strength, wisdom, contentment, peace, and happiness.

So I do not offer a yoga class with a rap beat, techno music, or even turban clad sitar players, but hopefully I can share the practice of yoga in a safe, non-threatening, non-judgmental environment that is accepting and welcoming to all. I hope that you can find your true yoga someday as well.

CHAPTER 21

Yoga in A Blizzard

I live in the Central Massachusetts area and am currently looking at snow falling outside my window again. For most people, the forecast of snow is tantamount to a major disaster. Store shelves empty as people stock up on essentials (chips, dips, snack and junk food). Favorite programs are pre-empted so that we can all gaze at a weather map with colored bands, prediction amounts, and large font warnings. Serious looking news anchors report on the same doom and gloom scenarios, turning it over to long suffering weather people who must pump enthusiasm into their reports over and over again. Have you ever wondered what those poor newscasters did that relegates them to the outside during these storms?

Snow and blizzards happen. It can be a nuisance, especially if the power goes out, and I am sympathetic to those who live in an area where the weather could destroy their property. I also have heightened awareness as to how the weather affects the services my elderly parents receive in their home and know that we must prepare in advance if meals on wheels cannot make their deliveries and make sure that there are plenty of their medications on hand. But like when I lived in Galveston, TX where hurricanes are a way of life and again in Seattle, WA, where there is the potential of earthquakes, preparation is key. So if you are warned and prepared, why not use yoga instead?

Use the yogic principle of Asteya(non-stealing) and Aparigrapha(non-hoarding) while preparing for the storm. Obviously, you are not going to steal food or other necessary items, but taking more than you need is unnecessary. How many bags of chips do you need? Before going out to shovel practice yoga asana to help gently warm up your body and stretch to avoid injury. Practice Seva (service to others) by checking on and perhaps extending your shoveling efforts to include your neighbors. I have a neighbor who has to be 80 if he is a day, and he takes great pride in being able to still maneuver his snow blower. I see him doing driveways of others, even neighbors on vacation! Finally, practice Santosha (contentment) as you watch the snow billowing and dancing around. It really is beautiful and peaceful. And believe me, as a teacher, it never gets old to have a " snow day"!

• CHAPTER 22 •

A Yoga Valentine For You

The month of February is known for Valentines, hearts, chocolates, and love. In yoga, your heart center is also known as the anahata chakra. Here is a Heart Center Meditation that you can do for yourself.

Heart Chakra Meditation

This heart chakra meditation is a simple technique to release sadness and fear and to bring compassion and love into your life. Sit in a comfortable position, either cross-legged on the floor or in a chair. Sit up tall with the spine straight, the shoulders relaxed and the chest open. Inhale the palms together and lightly press the knuckles of the thumbs into the sternum at the level of your heart (you should feel a little notch where the knuckles magically fit). Breathe slowly, smoothly and deeply into the belly and into the chest. Soften your gaze or lightly close the eyes. Let go of any thoughts or distractions and let the mind focus on feeling the breath move in and out of your body. Once the mind feels quiet and still, bring your focus to the light pressure of the thumbs pressing against your chest and feeling the beating of the heart. Keep this focus for one to five minutes. Next, gently release the hands and rub the palms together, making them very warm and energized. Place the right palm in the center of your chest and the left hand on top of the right. Close the eyes and feel the center of your chest warm and radiant, full of energy. See this energy as an emerald green light, radiating out from the center of your heart into the rest of your body. Feel this energy flowing out into the arms and hands, and flowing back into the heart. Stay with this visualization for one to five minutes. After you feel completely soaked with heart chakra energy, gently release the palms and turn them outwards with the elbows bent, the shoulders relaxed and the chest open. Feel or visualize the green light love energy flowing out of your palms and into the world. You can direct it towards specific loved ones in your life or to all sentient beings. To end your meditation, inhale the arms up towards the sky, connecting with the heavens, then exhale and lower the palms lightly to the floor, connecting with the earth. Take a moment or two before moving on with the rest of your day. I hope that you take the time to give yourself this Valentine and may you have abundant love in your life always.

• CHAPTER 23 •

5 Ways to Discover Yoga

(Published October 13, 2013)

Today is Columbus Day. It is the semi-holiday for selling things Columbus never ever imagined existed in his time. Don't you imagine what would have happened if old Chris had GPS or even radar? Anyway, the point of this holiday is not celebrating his mistake but rather his conviction and stubbornness to prove a point.

The one thing that was around during Columbus's time was yoga. It is doubtful that he and his crew practiced yoga or even heard of it but if they did they might have made a few more discoveries.

Here's what you can discover by starting (or continuing) a yoga practice:

1. How to calm the mind and body

Yogis know how to center themselves and learn to use their breath to bring blood flow and oxygen to the muscles. Yogis can find themselves in a serene place even amidst chaos around them.

2. How to be patient with oneself

Yogis learn that their bodies are ever changing and so what they may have done on the mat the week or day before might not be the same on the mat today. Yogis can tune out and go within. They honor their bodies and learn to adapt.

3. How to create intentions

Yogis learn how to set intentions in their lives. It might be as simple as "I am calm" or as complex as finding a new career.

4. How to reach beyond oneself

Part of the yogic principles includes doing seva or service. Yogis know that they are part of a community and everyone and everything is linked.

5. How to live yoga off the mat

Yogis know that yoga isn't just a Hollywood fad but a way of life. Yoga is something you do for your mind, your body, and your spirit.

Happy Columbus Day! I hope that you discover all that yoga has to offer you.

• CHAPTER 24 •

Yoga for Depression

(*Published August 13, 2014*)

The untimely passing of Robin Williams this week, brought home the very real effects of depression. According to the Center for Disease Control (CDC), about 9% of Americans have feelings of hopelessness, despondency, and/or guilt that generate a diagnosis of depression (http://www.everydayhealth.com). About 30,0000 Americans have depression severe enough that results in suicide. Obviously severe depression needs to be treated medically, but there are some preventative poses in yoga known to help depression.

For a type of depression that tends to make people brood or withdraw, vigorous asanas such as Sun Salutation (Surya Namaskar) will help stimulate the breath. The physicality of this asana challenges the body so the mind is focused on completing the poses, rather than the turmoil within. For the types of depression where people are restless, unfocused, and almost manic in their inability to control their thoughts, backbends are more helpful. These people find it very difficult to relax and remain still in Savasana or in a meditation and they might find that closing their eyes actually produces more anxiety. These people need to understand that the eyes do not have to be closed and relaxation can be achieved through a more supported or counter pose.

For more in-depth look at how depression can be helped with yoga, please see Yoga as Medicine by Dr. Timothy McCall.

Depression is a very real and insidious ailment and though it feels helpless, there is help available. In the U.S., call 1-800-273-8255 for National Suicide Prevention Lifeline. Please use social media for good and pass this along.

• CHAPTER 25 •

Back to School Yoga

This week many people are getting ready to go back to school. Whether you are a student, a teacher, or a caregiver for school age children, don't forget to bring yoga with you. Here are some benefits:

Yoga can relax your mind as well as your body. Simply taking deep breaths when you are nervous or stressed will help to lower your blood pressure and reduce anxiety.

Yoga can stretch the body. Taking the time to do some simple yoga stretches will help you feel renewed and refreshed. This is especially important if you are crammed into a desk for hours expected to think, create, and produce. You will find yoga will actually help with your work output.

Yoga aids your spirit. It brings you to a place of peace, which in turn, you bring to your dealings with others around you. What goes around will definitely come around in a good way!

My motto is: *Calm the mind, stretch the body and invigorate the spirit.* Try yoga!

· CHAPTER 26 ·

Yoga for Job Loss

(*Published 7-21-15*)

Summertime and my mind is not easy. For the second time in 19 years I am not filling my summer with professional development courses, curriculum updates, classroom refurbishment, and preparation for the new school year. The first time doesn't count as I was moving cross-country from the state of Washington to Massachusetts. This summer it is because I don't have a classroom to go to. It's unsettling. Suddenly my days are filled with trolling the education job boards, sending out resumes to a faceless electronic abyss, getting the same electronic rejection letters back, and finding solace with inspirational pictures and quotes on Facebook. Losing a job is right up there with other major life changes and it's not a comfortable place to be. Random thoughts start to intrude-anger, grief, loss, unworthiness, self-doubt-all of which are normal and should not be ignored. It's when these feelings start to overwhelm and manifest themselves into physical and mental blockages that you need to take action. Here's how yoga can help:

1. Start your day before you even get out of bed, setting an intention. It does not have to be a laundry list of chores, but it should be one thing you wish to accomplish. I like to link my breath with my intention, i.e. as I breathe in say to myself "I am" and as I breathe out state my intention.

2. **Be with people-even ones you don't know!** I find it's when I'm alone that I feel the worst, so I walk or get in the car and get myself to a public place. Talking to a random stranger about anything is better than talking trash about your situation when you are alone! And when that lady at Dunkin Donuts smiles at you or the librarian says, "Have a good day", it can change your mood.

3. **Take the high road.** It is so easy in this day and age when you can electronically skewer people and institutions you don't like or have a grudge against. Even if it is justified, you might feel vindicated momentarily but what goes around comes around-and that holds true for the people who got you into this situation to begin with.

4. **Practice a yoga pose.** Promise yourself that you will do it faithfully until you master it or want to move on to another. There are plenty of poses for relaxation, depression, stretching, and calming the mind.

5. **Plan out your job renewal.** Make a list for your perfect job and don't hold back! Create everything you want- location, responsibilities, hours, and money. Then list what you can realistically do to get it. Granted, job searches are not fair and there are many things beyond your control, but what can you control? What can you do to make your job manifest itself for you? Once you are certain exactly what you want, don't keep it a secret. Now is a good time to use Facebook and Linkedin and let people know how they can help.

It has been a month since I lost my job but in reality five months since I knew that my last job situation did not serve me, nourish me, or sustain me (except for my colleagues who are fantastic, hard-working, underpaid professionals!) I am using yoga for my job loss. Try it for yourself and let me know what you create!

CHAPTER 27

What is Yoga Nidra?

Think of a warm summer's day. You are sitting on a soft blanket. Your toes are extended into the pink sand. There is a gentle breeze. You hear the rhythmic sounds of the waves and see the sparkling blue ocean waters. The warmth of the sun penetrates into your tired bones and releases any tension or pain. You are suspended in a timeless cocoon of warmth, happiness, and carefree abandon. You are one with the universe.

This is Yoga Nidra.

Yoga Nidra is our conscious effort to relax and renex. In our yoga practice we stir up and activate our bodies and nervous systems. Yoga Nidra helps us to cool down and restore normal body temperature. It also helps us to meditate and practice Pranayama, the use of the breath and controlling the breath in yoga practice. Perhaps even reach the state of Pratyahara, or the bridge between, bringing awareness to reside deep within oneself. The goal of Yoga Nidra is to free the senses and rest in inner space.

Why is this good for you? The practice of Yoga Nidra can help to reduce stress, alleviate anxiety and calm the nervous system. It can help with insomnia, chronic pain, and emotional disorders. It has been used successfully with veterans suffering from PTSD and yogis who aspire to go deeper into their practice to reach Samadhi.

There are many ways to learn and practice Yoga Nidra through CDS, MP3s, and workshops. A form of Yoga Nidra, called Savasana, is practiced at the end of each instructor led yoga class. It may be hard to completely let yourself go, to quiet the mind, and let everything be at peace. Like everything else in your yoga practice, it takes time to feel comfortable doing this. Bring an eye pillow, snuggle under a warm blanket, and feel the weight of the world float away. Give yourself the gift of Yoga Nidra.

• CHAPTER 28 •

Being Thankful and Content!

"Rest and be thankful."—William Woodsworth

(Published November 24, 2013)

Thanksgiving is a day set aside to enjoy our many blessings-family, friends, food, and the things that make us feel happy and content. In yoga contentment is called santosha. Practicing this niyama is not a wimpy settling or being passive about life's circumstances, but rather enjoying what you have and have been given.

    I strive to make Thanksgiving a simple family holiday. For many years, my husband, children, and I lived 3,000 miles away from our immediate families. With not much money and little resources, we had to find joy in the little and cheap things like playing cards, eating Annie's macaroni and cheese (a big extravagance for us!), and making construction paper decorations. Even after we moved closer to our families, many years were spent supporting our children in the band by manning the concession stands at the local football games after which the last thing we wanted to do was eat a big meal. Now it is welcoming them home for a night or two from their busy lives and seeing a movie.

This year as I list my many blessings I count among them the fact that I have a job, a car that works, and students who enjoy learning as much as I enjoy teaching. I am thankful for my husband who endures a stressful job to provide us with financial and medical security. I am thankful that my parents are still alive and still living in their own home and grateful for my sister's help in managing their affairs. I am thankful that my children have jobs and can support themselves. I am thankful that my book (Yogaminute) is done and published. And I am especially thankful for my dog, who loves me unconditionally and is always happy to see me and be with me no matter what my mood.

What are you thankful for?

• CHAPTER 29 •

Don't Go Strapless in Yoga!

When I was training to be a yoga instructor, we would start off our sessions with a ninety minute asana practice. It was a wonderful way to start off the day and to learn the poses which we would then instruct to others. In one of the first training sessions I remember floating effortlessly into a Triangle Pose (Utthita Trikonasana) and relaxing into the side bend, reaching for my toes. I was so comfortable in the pose at first I didn't notice that someone was standing on either side of me and one of those people was holding a yoga strap and a block. Immediately my body tensed and then of course, I looked around to see who they were going to correct. Of course it was me! The reason I floated effortlessly was because my hips were out of alignment and my feet were not spaced correctly. Instructor One demonstrated how I was supposed to start off the pose. No problem as I immediately did what I did before-and was wrong. I stubbornly must have tried at least three times to get into that pose, all the while eying Instructor Two who was wordlessly holding the yoga props. Finally after the third time, Instructor One needed to adjust someone else and Instructor Two just stood wordlessly next to me holding the props.

My first thought was "What is wrong with me?" and my second was "Everyone must be looking at me!" and my third was "Oh my goodness, I'm not good enough to teach other people if I can't do it myself!" all in the matter of about three seconds.

Sensing all of this emotional turmoil, but still not saying anything, Instructor Two stood in front of me. She positioned herself on the outer edge of my mat, adjusted the strap around her foot, positioned the block and went into the pose. Then she came out of the pose and again, wordlessly, left the strap and block on my mat.

Well, OK, since she left it there, I guess I could try to do it her way. I attached the strap to my foot, positioned the block, and again went into the pose effortlessly, but this time it felt different. My stance was wider, my torso elongated, and my hand was positioned exactly so. I felt a different opening occurring within my body and it felt good because I was doing it correctly.

I am glad that this happened to me during my training. It allowed me to experience that in my yoga practice and to be truly happy, there is no ego. I realized that using a strap or a block or two does not mean I am not good enough or that I am cheating in some way. Rather, I would be cheating myself if I did not experience the benefits of the pose done correctly.

So next time you are practicing at the yoga studio or at home, let your mind and body be open to using props. It will only enhance and deepen your practice and your understanding of yourself.

• CHAPTER 30 •

Discounted Senior?

It was a lovely fall day. My husband and I took a ride to New Hampshire to visit the Reeds Ferry Shed Company (If you need a shed, check them out!). After our visit, we stopped to fill up the gas tank and while my husband was pumping I went across the street to Dunkin Donuts to get us some coffee. My parents owned and operated Anita's Donuts for over 20 years, and the smell of donuts and coffee brings back so many yummy memories for me. This day's memory may not be in the yummy category.

So anyway, I am in line and placed my order for two black coffees. The girl behind the counter asked the size and thankfully I didn't have to remember the quasi Italian Starbucks jargon and said regular.

"Do you mean medium?" the girl asked.

"Oh," I responded. "Medium, I guess. No large. Definitely two large coffees."

"You want regular coffee?" the girl asked.

"Yes," I responded thinking she meant the regular Dunkin blend rather than the fall inspired pumpkin blends.

But instead of rushing to get my coffee, the girl is now squinting at me. "You want regular coffee? With cream and sugar?" she asked.

"No, black coffee. Two large black coffees!" I said thinking I am speaking English here?

Another squint from the girl, as she announces my total, takes my money, and directs me to stand right where I am and she will bring me my coffees. Why, I am thinking, am I not directed to the pickup window? Obviously, other people are wondering this as well, based on the eye rolling and heavy sighs of the caffeine deprived patrons behind me.

Finally, my two coffees arrive and I exit the store to the gas station where my husband is waiting. It is on the way that I notice my receipt-

The girl gave me a senior discount!!!

Now, I am not opposed to discounts. I've been known to travel out of my way to save a few cents with discount and double coupons. But a senior discount? I admit I do have a few grays in my hair and a few stray whiskers on the chin but thanks to yoga my body has never looked better. Is it because of the conversation at the counter? Does confusion equal senior? Am I having too many senior moments and not realizing it? Am I now labeled a senior?

Not since I was called "Mam" have I been so taken aback. And the Mam thing occurred in Texas so I didn't even give that more than a second thought. I'm not even a grandmother yet!

So after my rants and raves and "What did she mean by that?" conversation (mostly to myself) my husband finally said,

"Maybe she hit the wrong key!"

OK. I can live with that. Sometimes I make mistakes and sometimes I forget names. I am active. I am still employed. I'm not losing my mind. I am not senile. And when I do hit that certain age when I could ask for a senior discount I'll take the cents off-but I won't be discounted!

Take that squinty eyed, Dunkin Donuts girl!

CHAPTER 31

Karma Yoga-Not Karma Sutra!

Way back in St. Luke's School, one of our favorite jobs and privileges was to carry around the "Mission Boy". This bronze statue was of a poor African boy with his hands wrapped around a small bowl. The idea was to "feed" the statue money. What was amazing to us in Kindergarten and First Grade (old hat by Second) was that he nodded his head every time you fed him coins. We couldn't wait to put our pennies into the statue!

Karma Yoga is known as the yoga of service. Not to be confused with the Karma Sutra (that's another kind of service!), Karma Yoga is selfless service (seva) for the good of humanity. There are some dedicated students of yoga whose mission is to extend this service around the globe. Organizations have been started and many have joined seeking to spread seva, into many locations.

This past week I held my first local Yoga For A Cause. This event was started in honor of my niece, who passed away from cancer only 6 months to the day she was diagnosed. She was a 29 years old, left a ten year old son and many of us who felt helpless in our inability to do anything but watch her pain, suffering, and deterioration. This event did not bring her back, of course, but it was my way of taking a negative and turning it into a positive. I am very grateful to the yogis who came out to support this cause and to help raise money for a local family in need. I plan to continue to offer this event once a month to promote seva.

I applaud all those students who travel to other countries and dedicate their time and talents to serve others. Being of service, or practicing Karma Yoga, does not mean you have to travel great distances or even do extraordinary things. Small acts of dedication and your offerings in terms of your means go a long way. I promise you, as the saying goes, your small act will return to bless you a hundred fold. I bet many of you are already practicing this form of yoga but never thought of it that way.

Thanks again to all those who came out to support the cause last week. I challenge my readers to start or join a cause of your own. Please write and let me know what causes you are involved in and perhaps we can share that as well. Blessings to all of you!

• CHAPTER 32 •

Yoga and McDonald's

(Published July 30, 2013)

So I am scrolling through my Facebook messages today and what do I see? A YouTube video of McDonalds is promoting yoga! Picture a serene park with about twenty people sitting in sukhasana (easy pose), complete with chin mudra (thumb and forefinger make a circle while the other fingers extend out), chanting a low hum. All of a sudden, their hum becomes an ecstatic yum as a picture of a McDonalds McNugget is flashed before them.

Immediately the online scorn and contempt started flying, with comments and messages mainly focused on the (lack of) nutritional content of the McNugget. The outrage ranged from mild to sacrilegious with a few unprintable comments.

Come on! There is nothing more mainstream than McDonalds. They are worldwide. They provide a service, they give back to the community, and now if they are promoting yoga, that makes them OK with me.

I don't remember the last time a piece of McDonalds food passed through my lips. I admit I do frequent their drive through for Newman's Organic Coffee (such a bargain at $1.00). Granted when my children were growing up I could count on one hand the number of times I let them near enough to even smell the place (side note: When my children were little we lived in the Seattle area so it was a good place to play out of the rain). I don't think my eating habits will change because of the video. But I do applaud them for it.

What next? Ohm tattoos in Happy Meals?

• CHAPTER 33 •

Sssh! I Do It Everywhere!

A few weeks ago I wrote a post called Being in Easy Pose When Your Mind Is Not. In it I talk about how hard it is to get centered enough to sit still, relax, and meditate. I gave a few tips on how to quiet the mind, but still some of you are having difficulty. So this is for you.

First of all, I hear you. I come from the generation that says women must do it all (Remember: I can bring home the bacon and fry it up in the pan?) Sitting still in my family was tantamount to being lazy. Add some Catholic guilt onto that, and I felt I had to be busy every second of the day, doing something, or I wasn't a good employee/daughter/wife/mother. I think that is why I was first attracted to aerobic activity. When I was doing and teaching aerobics, I didn't have time to think about anything else but trying to breathe! There was really no down time, except for maybe a three-minute stretch segment at the end. When I was younger, yoga was not attractive to me, not because of the asana (exercise) part, but because I had to be alone with my thoughts and myself. Couldn't, wouldn't do it!

Now that I am older I find I can be quiet with myself. I can meditate when I have to. I don't have to be in a yoga class to do it. I make it my right to take a minute or two whenever I need it to breathe, relax, center, and give myself positive affirmations. I do it while I'm still in bed, before I go to sleep or right when I wake up. I do it at a stoplight. I do it at the grocery store. I do it at work. Sssh! Don't tell my husband-I might do it during sex. The point is you do not need to be sitting in a pretzel-like position, on a mat, chanting ohm, with incense all around you.

So give it a chance. It won't be easy, but it will be worth it.

• CHAPTER 34 •

Being in Easy Pose When the Mind is Not

Summertime..and the living is easy. Yes, as of Friday we are officially in summer. Barbeques, beaches, hikes, fresh produce, sunning, napping, gardening and for me as a teacher, no tests to correct, lessons to plan, or committees to worry about.

In yoga, the first pose a student is introduced to is called sukhasana or easy pose. It is a cross-legged, upright, seated position. In easy pose an instructor will usually start class with centering. Centering is when you get to leave all your worries and troubles of the day behind and concentrate on breathing, relaxing, and for some, doing some great introspective work. But it is not easy when your mind is restless. For most, it is a time when everything that has happened or will happen seems to intrude. "I can't believe that e-mail I got from her today!" "Traffic is terrible. Maybe I should leave a few minutes early." " I wonder what's on Facebook." "I think I didn't close the kitchen window." "What shall I make for summer tonight?" And on it goes. We call this the monkey mind. It just chatters and chatters with no rhyme or reason, flitting from one thought to the next, like ADHD on overdrive.

Calming the monkey mind is not easy and for most of us, it takes concentrated effort. Sometimes it's just a matter of lengthening your inhalations and exhalations. Sometimes it helps to give yourself a pep talk before you start. For instance, give yourself a mantra word to repeat over and over again such as "Relax" or "Quiet" or "Breathe". All of your life's business will be there when you finish. Give yourself the gift of taking time for yourself. Then you'll be singing:

Sukhanasana-and the pose is easy

• CHAPTER 35 •

Bringing Yoga On Vacation

Toothbrush? Yes. Swim suit? Yes. Pajamas? Maybe. Yoga? Of course! Packing for your vacation does not have to weigh you down and neither should your workout. Consider adding a select group of yoga poses to your daily routine. Here's how!

Start with visualization

Vacations are meant to be relaxing but perhaps you are combining it with a family event, which could be anything but! Before you even start your trip, set an intention to find peace and renewal away from your daily routine. Visualize a happy, content, and smiling you. Couple that with your intention (i.e. I will take pleasure in..) as you take deep breaths.

Master Mountain Pose

2 hour delays during check-in? You won't be bothered in Mountain Pose. Stand tall, feet about hip width apart. Roll your shoulders up, around, and down. Let you hands fall loosely by your sides as you fully inhale and exhale. This is a pose of strength, which you will need lugging your carry on baggage through security.

Seated Twists

Sitting during long plane or car rides won't bother you if you get up and stretch at regular intervals. Every twenty minutes or so, add a seated twist as well. Start by sitting up tall in your seat, feet flat on the floor. Inhale as you lengthen the spine, exhale as you turn your torso to the right. If you have room, stretch your arms overhead and let them fall to the right as well. Staying on the right side, inhale and use your exhalations to go even deeper into your twist. Your head can be eye level, or looking down if you need to stretch your neck. Repeat on the other side.

Drink water

Staying hydrated is important anyway, but especially as you might be changing time zones, or consuming items not in your usual daily diet. Visualize the water refreshing and cleansing your body with each sip.

Start and End your day with 5 minutes of your favorite poses.

Your morning routine could consist of a few rounds of sun salutation, or a brisk mindful walk in your vacation environment. Literally stop to smell the roses, walk barefoot through grass or sand, or anything else you do not take the time to do at home. Take mental snapshots and add captions such as "Feeling the morning dew on my toes", "Frolicking in the waves", "Enjoying the sunset".

Say No!

Remember this is your vacation! Yes, you might have to do some compromising with your partner or family if you are not traveling alone, but be sure to set aside time to do the things you enjoy. In yoga this is called ahimsa, or speaking the truth.

Keep the vacation going by incorporating yoga into your daily life. A few minutes a day is all it takes!

CHAPTER 36

Olympic Lessons For The Rest of Us

(Published August 22, 2016)

Discipline. Dedication. Determination. These are the three descriptors that come to my mind when I think Olympic athlete. What we see is only a small snapshot of their sport; we don't see the tears, the disappointments, the missed social opportunities, and the sacrifices of their families and friends. What we see is a fleeting glimpse, oftentimes just a few seconds, of what it takes to be an Olympian. Sometimes it's triumphant; sometimes it's not.

I watched in awe the achievements of these men and women. For a few weeks, Simone, Ally, Michael, David, and many others became part of my family. I can't help but reflect on how these athletes overcame the physical and mental challenges of their sports. I can't imagine what pressure they were under with the whole world witnessing. I can't help but wonder in what direction their lives will turn now that the flame has gone out.

How can the common person, you and I, honor our Olympians? Use the achievements of these Olympics to define what and who you want to be. Change something that needs changing. Take a leap with no regrets. Release the past and create a new future. Take just one challenge and overcome it with the same inspiring, goal setting, and work ethic. Redefine what we see as an obstacle and reinvent it into a goal. Whether it is career, family, relationships, and yes, your yoga practice, all of us can use the Olympics as a model. I challenge you to challenge yourself.

• CHAPTER 37 •

Preparing for (A) Fall in Yoga

(*Published October 12, 2016*)

It is now officially Fall when we prepare our homes and ourselves for the winter months ahead. How can yoga help? As yogis, we know how yoga can help us physically, mentally and spiritually. As we dive deeper into our practice, we invite ourselves to change with it. Sometimes, these changes are not what we expect. Often times, being open to change can also lead us down the path of pain, disappointment, and rejection. It far more comfortable to shut ourselves away from people and situations outside our comfort zone, staying in our little hobbit holes of complacency. Yet when you are stagnant in one place, negative feelings will eventually percolate and bubble over. How long can you be ignored, marginalized, and taken advantage of before you become bitter, depressed, and robotic? I always tell my students who are new to yoga that the hardest poses they will do is centering at the beginning of class and savasana at the end because in these poses you are forced to be quiet and to look within.

So how can yoga prepare you for what lies ahead?

First, it is helpful to know that you are not alone. In this age of social media, there is always someone or some group out there who you can connect with (in a safe way of course). Isn't it true that being anonymous is so much more freeing than being face to face? Just remember to use common sense when posting, getting and listening to advice.

Second, change isn't all bad. You can always take "baby steps" if the change is within your control, go with your gut, and don't second-guess yourself. You are your best teacher.

Finally, yoga is made to help you navigate changes. Listen to your breath, listen to your body, and follow your heart. Be open to the changes within. Let yoga be your guide.

• CHAPTER 38 •

Practicing Kindness

(Published November 15, 2016)

Kindness towards yourself and others is not an easy thing to do. Reflecting on your use of time, how often does kindness figure in? Can you go just a few minutes without letting negative thoughts come through? As a teacher in an elementary school and as a yogi, I hope to model kindness in my everyday actions, yet I realize that there are some days when it is a struggle, when it is easy and convenient to deflect blame or wallow in negative thoughts.

A few weeks ago my mother passed away. In that time I have been the recipient of so many kind acts that it humbles me. I'd like to acknowledge some:

- Nashoba Valley Hospital volunteers in Ayer who supplied coffee and snacks while we were sitting with my mom.
- Kelleye, the nurse on duty, who explained the end of life process to us, checked in without being obtrusive, and stayed passed her shift to give my dad a hug.
- Neighbors and relatives who brought food, sent cards, and sat with us
- Neighbors and friends who went to visit and sit with my dad after everyone went back home to their lives
- People I work with who came to the wake, sent me messages and cards, and

Jeff who baked delicious bread when I returned to work

- People who know me from my yoga practice, blog, and Facebook, who sent words of encouragement.

Thank you for your kindness. Kindness received becomes kindness given. Perhaps in the aftermath of this election, our leaders can practice that as well.

CHAPTER 39

It's Not OK!

(Published January 6, 2018)

Many of you who follow my posts know that I advocate to use yoga to stay healthy in mind, body, and spirit. I use yoga Asana (the physical part), along with Pranayama (the breathing part), as well as the introspection of Svadhyaya, to promote spiritual health. What I have been remiss in writing about is acknowledgement and that's not OK.

To acknowledge a hurt and a disappointment, even privately, is frowned upon. Children are told, "Don't be a baby"; teens are told, "Grow up"; and adults are told to "Handle it", or "Be a team player". Acknowledgement is not advocated until it becomes out of control.

It's not OK to bury resentment and disappointment. It's not OK to let someone or something control you. It's not OK to be mistreated, maligned, and managed. It's not OK to say you're fine when you're not.

I applaud the women and men who are part of the *#metoo* movement that is now coming to light. They have shown courage in making their stories so public and I hope the media attention will help them feel vindicated and released from their burden. But what of the people who carry a hurt every day and have no outlet to express it? To those people I say give yourself permission to acknowledge. Write it down, say it out loud, tweet or text it if you want. You have the right to be heard and acknowledged. Not everyone will see it your way, and you might not get the sincere, contrite reaction you are expecting, but just the act of acknowledgement will help you towards the road to healing.

- I acknowledge the people and institutions that were unkind and dismissive to me.
- I acknowledge the clients and potential employers who did not hire me.
- I acknowledge that my body is not 20 anymore.
- I acknowledge that there are things out of my control.

What do you acknowledge? *#Metoo*

• CHAPTER 40 •

Can You Really Be Thankful?

There is a commercial currently running that features a group of guys in a convertible, running low on gas. One of the guys takes out a birthday card from the glove compartment, takes a picture of the enclosed check, and voila! They can instantly buy the gas they need and are on their way. Clearly they are happy for both the gas and the instant access to the funds. But are they truly thankful?

Little children everywhere are taught to say please and say thank you, and they dutifully repeat these words to get the object of their desire, but we know they are just parroting the words. They do not hold meaning, other than it makes the adults smile, and that is good in their little world.

In our everyday life, we routinely say thank you as well. It is polite, socially acceptable, and a conversation ender. You said it, it's done, on to other things. But saying thank you and feeling thankful are two separate things.

When I think of the times that I have been truly thankful, it is because someone shared his or her skill or resources to help me do something I could not do myself. Whether that was a doctor, a fire fighter, a technician, an auto mechanic, a teacher, a co-worker, or a stranger, the times I am truly thankful is when I am in need. I am even more thankful when I see what it costs for the giver to help me. How many of us have received checks in birthday cards from a grandparent or older relative? How many of us realize the actual cost to those sending the check? Do the guys in the commercial think about what grandma went without so she could send a $10.00 check (plus postage?)

Saying thank you is easy. Being truly thankful requires humility, sincerity, and empathy. In our yoga practice, we focus on these things and seek to stay on our path of enlightenment. What are you truly thankful for today? How can you show it?

Pay it Forward in kindness and truly celebrate the Thanksgiving holiday in your mind, in your words, and in your heart.

ALSO AVAILABLE

STRESSED? CAN'T SLEEP? FEEL OVERWHELMED?

Get Yogaminute-Got a minute? You can do yoga!

This easy to follow guide is for **anyone** who needs to incorporate yoga into his or her daily live, one minute at a time. Simple instruction, pictures of real people, and lots of yoga poses make this book the one to get! Available on Amazon and Barnes and Noble.com.

ABOUT THE AUTHOR

Anita Perry is an author, educator, yogi, and blogger with close to 40 years in the health industry. She provides yoga instruction and inspiration for groups, individuals, corporate, and school settings. Ms. Perry is the author of Yogaminute and a frequent guest wellness speaker.

www.ingramcontent.com/pod-product-compliance
Lightning Source LLC
LaVergne TN
LVHW051559070426
835507LV00021B/2657